Beyond the Bitter Wind

Beyond the Bitter Wind

Poems 1982–2000

CHRISTOPHER SOUTHGATE

Shoestring  Press

Typeset by The Midlands Book Typesetting Company, Loughborough (01509 210920)
Printed by Quorn Selective Repro Loughborough (01509 213456)

Published by Shoestring Press
19 Devonshire Avenue, Beeston, Nottingham, NG9 1BS
Telephone: (0115) 925 1827

First published 2000

ISBN: 1 899549 47 1

east midlands
arts
making creative
opportunities

Shoestring Press gratefully acknowledges financial assistance from
East Midlands Arts

To my parents, fifty years married

ACKNOWLEDGEMENTS

Acknowledgements are due to the editors of the following publications in which a number of these poems, or versions of these poems, first appeared: *Christian, The Coffee House, The Collins Anthology of New Christian Poetry, The Company of Poets Anthologies 1, 2, 3, 'Taboo', and 'Exposing the Negatives', Connections, Critical Survey, Encounter, Envoi, The Frogmore Papers, The Interpreter's House, The Middlesex Full Circle Prize Anthology 1999, Orbis, Otter, The Oxford Magazine, Paris Atlantic, Prospice, Sepia, Smith's Knoll, The South Coast Poetry Journal, South West Poetry Competition Prize Anthology 1993, The Swansea Review, A Time of Singing, Westwords,* and *The Yellow Crane.*

The completion of this manuscript was enormously assisted by the award of a Hawthornden Fellowship in 1999. I also thank many poet colleagues, and Richard Skinner in particular, for years of careful responding to work in progress. My wife Sandy has nurtured my poem-making since its beginning; no words are enough for thanks to her.

I do however want to express my particular gratitude to John Lucas for his enthusiasm for the work, his searching editorial pencillings, and all his support in seeing the book through to publication.

Other books of poetry by Christopher Southgate

Landscape or Land? Poems for Devon (with Mark Beeson) Wheal Press, 1989

Annotations: Selected Early Poems Parfordwood, 1991

A Love and its Sounding: Explorations of T.S.Eliot (a verse biography of the poet, with companion essays) University of Salzburg, 1997

Cover photograph of Scorhill, Dartmoor, by Frankie Fraser
Photograph of the author by Gordon Couttie

Contents

I. THE MIND IS ITS OWN PLACE

The mind is its own place, and in itself
Can make a heaven of Hell, a hell of Heaven.

John Milton, *Paradise Lost*

DESTINATION

I use the moor today, ashamedly,
as an antidote
to blind family anger.

I start the long slope of Hameldown
(the far ridge like a line
of scripture, forbidding self-love).

Wind against. A white film dusting
the kists. Deer-sprites
seem to haunt the valley-floors.

The sky is empty, wash-blue, as though
some controlled explosion
had cleared away its debris

leaving only light, and three thorn
trees, absolute
as to sharpness. Suffering.

The snow's striations are intricate,
seem hand-turned;
melt-pools dissolve my eyes.

I find rest in hard ascent, my chaos
left printed in the white,
false summits disregarded.

As I stump down off the hill the snow
drifts after me, erasing
my working. I walk away empty –

begin again today, apparently,
but feel somehow foreknown,
like that new-etched scimitar of moon.

WRITERS' MORNING

(after John Donne)

Blustery air rattles the window-catch
to wake us, surprises me till I remember –
warm enough, at last, to leave open
windows that were always flung wide
at night in childhood holidays.
And I hear again childhood's first
summer wood-pigeon, wind through great trees,
first sneeze coming, of new-mown Devon.

This morning then spans time – I think
of telling you, think better, hold you,
touch gold at the nape of your neck.
For joy I want to stop time, arrest
the copper beech leaves at their hue
of young Beaujolais, and the reddish sun at the angle
at which it first catches our neighbour's new thatch.

I do not want to change the status
of the extreme peace of holding you
or of the impatience I know is coming;
you'll goad me out of bed and I'll pretend
not to be glad to make fresh coffee, and take
a fresh white page to stare at.

I savour in advance tiredness –
filled page, flavour of your newest song –
violet and indigo after the setting sun.
I dread our 'undoing' epitaph, yet death
which is also in this moment gives
to every breath before we get to work
its intensity. In your arms I am child
and widower remembering.

I start to rise, ready to be busy.
You move your fair and tousled head,
half-sleeping still, call out.
I fall back, time-stopped,
in wonder at the song of you.

SHE'S HIS MIRANDA

She's his Miranda, his always-to-be-adored,
though he's never told her
and she's married to another,
has three children and a cat.

He
        always sees her at the edge of a glade
in the half-light, the lustre of her eyes
compelling him. He is leopard, as well as prince.

She
        worries about negative equity,
schools' league tables. Yearns
simply for company.

He cannot guess by what wizardry
he still loves her.

She cannot see why it must always
be so difficult between them.

They meet
in the glare of children's questions,
partners' watchfulness.

To him she is as much a quality
a conviction formed out of strong air,
as a person. He replays endlessly
their first few meetings. Their only dance.

Recently the realisation.
It would have been he
who would have been unfaithful.

CLARITY

Well, things have clarified themselves.
I always knew, I suppose,
That he loved me. I hate
To sell the flat, though.
But it *is* a good time.

Things have clarified themselves.
The fact of the child, I mean.
It makes it all plain.
Of course it'll hurt Peter
But he *has* his work.

Things have clarified themselves.
Relief to us all. The paperwork,
Though. They wrote every day
When they were engaged. Probate
Will be through soon. No, I'm *not*.

Things have clarified themselves.
So helpful at the clinic. So
Good to be able to use
The words. No, I don't think
He'll ever. I'm afraid so. For *years*.

Well, things have really clarified themselves,
I think. I'll have to .. no, I'm
Not right. Was *that* what they..
One of *those* places. Oh, no,
No, I'd rather die.

LISTENING

I listen to him in the College Bar,
On the motorway in the GTI,
In the take-away. His words are like
Backhands, well-coached, striking
The practice wall at the approved height –
Always rebounding.
The set of his eyes, tearless,
Determined, speaks of the soft, certain
Click of lawyers' doors.

I listen to her in the rain,
On the Circle Line, at a deserted
Exhibition of etchings. Her words
Are like the cries of a swallow
Caught in a church. She skims issues;
She has always lived by instincts.
Her eyes, mobile, elude offices,
Counsel instead integrity,
Silence, unchargeable time.

I listen, and both of them convince.
They have more courage than I
Would ever have. They show
Each other's postures for false
And self-seeking. They point back
To uncorrupted hours – birdsong
Bursting out of spring mornings,
Long days of love-play. It was only
The other's fear that was impractical.

I listen because if I once speak
My words will be the lies.

A COLD GEOMETRY

Three is an awkward number for a candlelit
Dinner. It breeds a cold geometry
In which the best of lights seems contrived.
The losing knight strives to bluff out
Disaster, but finds his rival baldly testing him
With shallow questioning. A lout.
Quite unworthy. What seemed fluent in her
Becomes awkward, gritty falsehood: what now
Safe, the luxury of hating her, slides
As the evening begins to quicken away from him,
Spraying wineglass tinklings around his anger,
Into the chiller security of love.

The candles gutter. He lets the talk trace its track,
The health of relatives she used
To come with him to visit, the state of arts.
He waits for perfect words – farewells
That will leave the rival's presence empty,
Their continued conjunctions banal
Against the snow-light of silent, implicit devotion.
The parting comes in slush, is brief,
Incapable of misremembering.
Having arrived grandly by taxi
He sets out to walk his way home, cold,
Alone, miscounting the Pleiades.

SPELLS

It's just the same – things haven't changed at all,
Annette said sadly, at dinner at a friend's,
the spell you weave is still the same old spell.

I wish you hadn't come, she said. I was doing so well
without you. So typical of you, not to understand.
You're just the same – you haven't changed at all.

If I'd known, I could have tried to cancel,
or been ready to ignore you. But why pretend?
The spell you weave is still the same old spell.

Soon after that I overheard her tell
her host she couldn't stay. She kissed me hard, and said again,
it's just the same – things haven't changed at all.

I almost loved her then, seeing another effort to disenthral
herself had come to such a fruitless end.
The spell I weave is still the same old spell.

That night I hear that Kate's in town. I call.
I drop everything, for the awkward hopeless hour we'll spend.
I'm just the same – I haven't changed at all.
The spell she weaves is still the same old spell.

RUNNING ON ICE

A dream. I run across a frozen harbour.
If I keep moving, don't look to either side
I don't lose touch with the ice-path, don't sink
into the lightless water. I can guide
my thoughts into surfaces, into talk
that places no weight, never asks the why
of running feet.
                                    What if a blizzard
covers the path? What if my lover should die?
They say depression, in men, can lead to frenzied
immersion in a wide variety of tasks.
Not me. I dream of running on ice, wake early,
drive to work, wear out a million masks.

THE MASTER'S TALE

Forty years ago,
New boy at the College feast,
He listened to the great men of the day,
Jokingly, over walnuts,
Drafting each other's obituaries.

He made a sustained contribution,
Writes EG. For which
We must all be thankful,
Writes IE. After a short illness,
Gallantly faced. DSP.

Yesterday, a CAT scan of the Master's brain.
Slight strokes, and atrophy.
Today, the funeral of the oldest Fellow.
The Master manages the well-chosen words.

He sends to the cellars for the port he ordered
At his admission. He holds a party
For the kaleidoscopic young.

Seeing him listen, they tell him
The latest email virus, and the merits
Of pistachio-flavoured Haagen-Dazs.

One girl, braver than the rest,
Offers in parting that his house is gloomy -
All portraits of dead Masters.

When he wakes he finds he wants
To send her flowers. To give
Her lunch, in some light and easy place.

He cannot remember.
That day or the next or the next.
He cannot remember her name.

The College Steward, all disapproval,
Takes the portraits down.
The Master scans each one in turn

Searching for a gallant face.

SOMETIMES YOU ARE THE SUN

Sometimes you are the sun
lighting up the rocks' mourning.
You make every block and facet shine;
answer my deepest yearning.

Sometimes you are the cloud
hanging over the hills like the smoke
of a thousand quenched fires.
My hope does not penetrate your look.

Today you were the sun
glimpsed behind a smear of fogged gold.
You were the sun, white, heatless, far;
between us, mist seeped and swirled.

Tonight you are a brilliance of sudden meteors
in the branches of an old ash.

ADOLESCENT LEOPARD

For my stepson, at thirteen (1982)

He has the walk
The ranging stride of the adolescent leopard
He begins to have the stare:
Hard eyes fix on me under flat-groomed hair.
I, unaccustomed to such snarling,
Stilling my spirit, a pool of moonlight,
Shatter as he splashes
At evening wallow.

I have a few more years to give to him.
Then he'll lope with the other
Well-groomed college cats
In late-eighties analogues of alligator shirts,
Stalking his first Porsche.
I'll watch in some hard-milled security,
Remember stride and snarl, and only then
Admit to loving him.

VARIATION IN A REMOTE KEY

I've not been myself recently
Though I see myself – routinely –
Striding from Engineering down the path
To Social Science – as I see also the heron
Spearing life out of the pretty ponds.

I've not been myself recently.
A stranger took my last slice
Of hard-earned leave, slept with my wife,
Enjoyed it, but he does not savour
Autumn the way I used to
Or give time enough to Bach.

He is, typically, in three meetings at once:
The one in which he sits, owlishly,
Feigning wisdom, the previous one
In which he cast my veto, and the next,
Which he'll chair, recycling skills
I could once rejoice in.

Can I banish him? Theoretically.
Tell him to take his trite remarks,
His clanging incantations, off
Past Student Loans, and down
The leafstrewn valley.

His odd, cloying presence
Grows on me, though.
If I cast him off
It might after all turn out
To be winter.

'ZWEMMERS, 1942'

for my mother

A book of poems. Pages yellowing.
On the first in faded fountain pen
Your name, and 'Zwemmers, 1942'.
A cleanness to that –
Twenty-one, down from Cambridge,
You pick out poetry – perhaps
A print of Piero della Francesca.
Probably you stay at your club,
Cut the pages there, raid the verses
With the intensity of unrequited love.

A closer look – other colours
In the scene. Wartime. Zwemmers
Trading despite the Blitz, Cambridge
Denuded of its young men.
The Paddington train inches west,
Its blacked-out compartments
Beaded with the glow
Of nerve-steadying cigarettes.
And your own fear is there,
Of life lived without meaning.

Fifty years on. Your best poured out
On husband and children. Zwemmers
Are at the Courtauld now –
I pass by their branch, raid the Gallery
For cadences. Van Gogh with bandaged ear,
Stretched sensuality
In a Modigliani nude. My fear?
Of mediocrity. Mocked by Gauguin's
Giving maidens, by the good cheer
Of Cézanne's peasants at their cards.

Your brain scan today. I block out
A new fear, ask with studied voice
'Will you tell us the result?' And hear
'I may do'. Piero, after all,
In your calm committed reserve.
Your book of poems is like you,
Intense, not yielding easily
Its meaning, and my love
For your life no less strong
For being left thus unrequited.

FOR MY FATHER

The characteristic pose is strong:
Shoulders thrown forward, head driving
Your pen (letters schooled to smallness
By a First taken on rationed paper) -
Or that same head halted in mid-word,
Throwing out argument with Churchillian
Force. So strong I forget too easily
That you made my first bookcase, lavished
Hour after hour in the garden, teaching
Me courage, technique against leg-spin.

If I once remember, a flood of gifts
Pours in. Shame fires, fast as spilled ether
Firing across a laboratory bench, and acrid
Smoke out of the past clouds judgment I
Patiently polished on book after book.
Easier not to recall your parenthood.
Easier to be a second version of you -
Writing wilder, casting less good bronze,
Pausing, thrilled by power in an argument,
Shoulders thrown towards the expectant page.

MUNICH

"The time was not in all respects well chosen"
Churchill of Chamberlain visiting Hitler in 1938

In our family the two syllables – Munich –
were purely and simply short
for appeasement. Coming here
is a surprise – the monuments
ignore the whole of Nazidom
as if it had never been.
We visit the Toy Museum,
admire the rise of German science,
taste wine at the Residenz.
Only at the bottom of the glass
does it casually surface
that Hitler must have drunk here,
that the handsome Hofgarten
once hung with hooked flags.

In my family's wars I was quiet,
taking the measure of conflict.
In my work I am a mediator
and taste often of the heady
spiced wine of peace-making.
I hide other sides of me –
halls of Field-Marshals,
the herd desire to split sky,
an oh-so-sly search for scapegoats.
In the Munich story I am
Chamberlain certainly, and a conspirator,
and I hold out the gold-nibbed pen,
hand shaking with lust for history;
Hitler takes it and signs.

In the Munich Toy Musuem
are the biggest teddy bears
I have ever seen, clockwork
acrobats, station-masters
of splendid period railways,
and model soldiers of many countries,
the good guys and bad guys
of families.

II. TRANSCRIPTIONS

SOCRATES MEETS THE IMAGE CONSULTANTS

He was well-educated, we felt,
but had problems with self-worth,
claiming to know nothing.
We are used to more confidence
in ex-military men. Packaging,
too, was a difficulty – a certain
street-corner look, a roving eye.
Not that we have morals as such,
but these things have to be noted.
He bothers people, reads no paper,
in these (what shall we say now?).
oligarchic times, when the popular
will is easily manipulated,
he seems vulnerable.

I had seen them before, their sort.
I had not thought to find them
so respectable, the teachers of tricks –
how to stand, how to laugh,
how recline after a power lunch,
how to give a business kiss.
They sell style, and the beautiful
youth come and buy, just as before.
I tried to talk to one or two,
but style seems to make them resistant
to disinterested love.
This is a sadder age even
than I knew, and more dangerous.
I was gladdened only by this,

the unaccepting ferocity
of the women.

FRAGMENT

The fragment of Sappho numbered 31 ends with the phrase
'All must be endured, since even a poor man..'

Even a poor man
May look upon your lean limbs,
Ears humming, eyes sea-green
With desire. And sadness
At the waste of it.

Even a poor man
May fan-letter your fountaining fame,
Pen shaking, remembering,
Ruefully, equality,
And the taste of you.

Even a poor man
May babble, after the beep, a half-blown
Hope-message, love-poem
Of longing. 'Hardly,
Dear, the place for it'.

Even a poor man
Must cede success to Sappho – she
Who hears your lovely laughter seems to be
Like a man, like a sea-storm blustering
Across the face of you.

But all must be endured, for
Even a poor man
Sure only of being poor
Can have his heart healed
By forgetfulness, mat empty,
Phone silent, never waking up
To the grace of you.

LENT '88 – CRYING FREEDOM

written after seeing the film 'Crying Freedom' on
the day two British soldiers were trapped in an IRA funeral

The film primes opinions. Freedom
Is our cry. The long body, prone, brown,
Is Biko. The policemen are evil.
There is a plea in our hearts for pardon
For the complicitous six of Sharpeville.
We want the Afrikaaners to lose at power-tennis –
Their guns and riot-shields will not protect
For ever. In time they will go under.

The photograph, next morning, is of Ulster.
The body, no actor's, supine, bloody,
Is a British soldier's, torn
At a political funeral, like Biko's.
There is revenge in our hearts, against
Any who were in that riot. We want
Better shields, effective police. The SAS.

There is too much leisure for opinion
In our English flower-gardens.
Our hearts riot; the words in them
Tangle, like ornamental ivy –
Justice, lust, compassion, Barabbas.
We are at the worst station of the Cross –
The one at which we feel our reflexes fail.

DANDOLO'S BONES

Enrico Dandolo, Doge of Venice, led the Fourth Crusade in the sack of Constantinople in 1204, and was later buried in the city.

On a cruise to Constantinople
A couple of eightysomethings dance together
Like willow branches relaying
Long-remembered breeze.

I tell you: I hope I'll be like that
When I'm old.
Then read of Dandolo, blind and almost ninety,
Leading a blast of Crusaders
Against the ancient walls.

Triumph, some called it, or sacrilege,
It all depended. Terrible as thunder,
Making for ever his mark on the world.
Our aged pair switch to the cha-cha.

The great Doge chose to lie finally
In a ceremonial chest (stamped,
No doubt, with the splendid Markan lion)
In the gallery of the Hagia Sophia.
The world would know forever Dandolo,

Stormer of the unstormable,
Whereas the mark of the dancers on my retina
Is gone in a moment. Leaves fall,
May or may not rise again.
It all depends.

With the coming of Islam the bones
Of Dandolo were thrown, by order
Of the Sultan, to the city's dogs.

THE ARCHAEOLOGICAL MUSEUM, PIAZZETTA DI SAN MARCO, VENICE

Four halls of classical sculpture. Alone.
If she'd come I'd have shown her this style
And that one, and that, the archaic smile,
The school of Phidias, Praxiteles, Myron,
Filled still, Pentelic air with noisy theory,
Seen nothing, heard my own unwisdom. Instead
She sleeps on Torcello, the lovely, languid head
Still, her form a fallow line of poetry.

I breathe the stone in utter quiet, and learn.
Her eyes, unguessable jades, dream distrust;
The trust, the love, is in the sleeping – lust
For Aphrodite's light allowed, I turn
To Venice, watered sun on stone arrayed,
Gain curved, carved time – space to prefer jade.

SENTENCES

'Will we ever be finished with this law and this secret police between us?'
Jacques Derrida – *The Post Card*

The law between us
is that I
should never exacerbate your fear
and that you
should never expose
the thinness of my heroism.

The secret police enforce it well.

What if there were a coup?
What if the crazy music when we met
should escape the glass cases on the wall?
What if our words were plain to one another?
Then we would be in the bush at nightfall –
hearing the leopard's cough, hyena howl,

and, cupped in the palms of drumming hands,

the soft slap of the Holy Ghost.

THE PRACTICE ROOM

Standing outside the green door
Every twenty past four, I long
To break in on you, to taste
The waters of the moon-dim lake
Ebbing and flowing as the notes
Under the left hand. I am impatient
Of the way you modulate your life –
Of all that time in the practice room –
And long to save you.

I grow fed up with *Mondschein*
And tell you so, in our seminar
On counterpoint. Your smile
Is a surprise – not the *Appassionata*
I'd longed to hear you play
Naked, while I made leaping fire
Out of unpromising kindling. I'd wanted
The lake to boil, I'd wanted to cut you off
Under sheer cliffs, under thunder-rolls.

****

In eleven years we have aged
A hundred opus numbers. The last quartets
Stalk around the house. When you play
It is the thirty-three variations
On a waltz by Diabelli. Obsessively.
We have moved into a late phase –
Full of dark colours and brilliances,
Full of brittle tone, hard on the technique.
Your eyes burn, after you have played.

Tonight I hear you crying
And cannot open the door
I painted green when we moved.
You have locked the door again,
Trapped us in the open
Under the lake-mad moon
With crazy old Beethoven –
Our Prometheus, and the eagle,
And the rock we are chained to.

THE MUSE SEEN IN A WINDOW

In a cold light, threatening rain,
the young art students are sent out
to sketch facades. Two I pass,
back to back, talking, the one
addressing the Cathedral (West Front),
the other the Deanery Yard,
a straggle of skyline
sheltering under South Tower.
They work fast, exchanging love-affairs.

I sit to write about them, in a café
chosen at random. I have fallen
in love with all of them, with their
sketchbooks of seriousness, unsustained,
with their laughter under the heavy sky.
I drug myself, *café et marc* – to exploit
this love for line and decorative
feature, and as I sink, maudlin
into my sublimate, I am sketched

by the most earnest of them all, gold-rimmed,
intent. To speak to her would be to cheat
on the twenty-year gap between us. I want
to buy her drawing with my poem, but
she moves round, takes me,
the neon sign and the drainpipes,
from our less flattering side, showing our age.
After that brief collusion the Muse
dispenses with her rival.

She hovers in the plate-glass light
when the student is gone.
As I scribble I am her gauche innocent
capturing a facade in a callow frame.
I strain to catch what she is writing,
but my reflection defeats me. I notice only
that she has aged well –
still winsome, *simpatica*, mocking
the efforts of her admirers.

A MIDDLE-AGED POET FACED WITH TITIAN'S 'THREE AGES OF MAN'

Do not put me on the right – with the infants,
Idiotic Michelin cherubs,
With never a thought in their wings.

No, not on the left either, with the young lovers:
Lazes on the damp grass go straight,
These days, to my lumbago.

Yet I am not at all ready for the company
Of the bald man behind, who ruminates long
On the decline in his ability to juggle skulls.

Rent me a space, at some reasonable fee of years,
In the background, observing babes and lovers,
Keeping company with that small deer

So sleek, possessed of such clarity in his stillness,
Poised always to escape me, and
Already, I see, in his winter colours.

CORRIDORS

A negative of a library.
A concrete cast of the space between shelves.

On guard an urbane woman
dressed in suit and mobile phone.
No sound comes from her
but the clicking
of her computer mouse.

I sit and stare at the anti-shelves,
still and remote as the Parthenon.
A kind of anti-conversation
develops between me
and the woman.

I am not buying.
I have not developed a whim
to convert one of my many stable-blocks
for the accommodation
of the anti-books of Rachel Whiteread.

Somehow the woman senses this.

She is not selling.
It would be an affront
to that white linen shirt
those perfectly organised cuffs
even to suggest it.

I make no suggestion.

While she clicks I scribble
in my notebook. It becomes
unthinkable that either should speak.
If her phone would go
I could catalogue her by accent, background.

If she scanned my notebook
all too much of my fear
would enter her data-set.
We sit. The concrete's breathing
leaves no mist on etched glass.

At last the anti-shelves volunteer
that there are truths to know
about deletion.
That violence can be
very precise.

The making of this cast
destroyed the books,
left a fossil, beautiful,
chill as a snow-wind
through the corridors of Dachau.

I get up and go. The woman and I
know all we need to know.

Rachel Whiteread's 'Book Corridors', a cast of the spaces within a library, forms part of a sequence which will culminate in the Holocaust Memorial for Vienna.

MASACCIO'S EVE

from the fresco of 'The Expulsion from the Garden' in the Capella Brancacci, Florence

Adam's distress we recognise;
It is a strong minor chord for all instruments –
Sustained, grieving, not looking at even
The possibility of modulation,
But all of a weave with itself.
Perhaps it is that in his heart
He is able to blame the woman
While still accepting his own victimhood.

For Eve young Masaccio – early twenties,
Hardly launched on his career –
Has found a note of far vaster desolation.
Or not one note exactly, but all the notes that come
When bows are drawn slowly across strings
Held away into dissonance.
So slow the drawing that every unevenness in the surface
Of each bow sets up its own grating.

It is in her body, yes, and in the unfeeling
Clasp of hands to breasts and groin –
Hands that deny there can ever again be bodily joy.
But most of all the torment is in the eyes –
Auschwitz eyes – five hundred years too early.
How does a Masaccio, a Mozart,
Make that move, start such dissonance
Running, as stretches spirits to new spaces of strain?
Who is the other who walks so close
into the unfamiliar land?

TWO ANNUNCIATIONS BY EL GRECO

Venice c.1570

I call you, from middle air,
Across a neat checked marble floor.
The Lord God has made his illegal
Move – he takes player-status
In humans' chess with sin.
His Holy Spirit, holding altitude,
Awaits your virgin turning gaze.

Toledo c.1600

I stand by you, on rock the colour
Of cloud, and admire courage. You
Are already looking up, praying,
As the Spirit sweeps towards us
Dove-formed but flaming –
Your face is flame,
The stone I stand on tomb-sized.
A bush takes fire.

THREE DESERTED WIVES

(after TS Eliot's 'Journey of the Magi')

A cold coming they had of it, we heard,
And were glad. We'd not been consulted,
But it gave us a chance to deal
With the silken girls.
For the first time to know
Equal meeting.

We learned the flute together,
Sat in a triangle of tents,
Complacent with shapelessness, swayed
By songs of bitter queens.
In succession of days
There was healing.

We learned that a graceful circle
Was pleasing in its own right.
We danced gravely, sweeping
Shawls to the Mother of all.
In growth of new incense-trees
There was power.

Wizened women of the country
Were our diviners. The old questions
Could be safely disregarded,
Weeds in our well-tended garden.
At night we danced wild,
Each a different creature.

The earthquake in the north mountains
Laid flat the new plain palaces
Where we had sought to centre,
Scattered camels, beat at faith.
Stereotyped, we nursed
Resented wounded.

They returned at last, bringing us
No presents. They spoke of birth,
Which we had given them, and death -
Already heavy on the ochre air.
Questions of lordship hummed
On northern hills.

Our flutes are cracked now, and played
Only to chide children. We meet
At night, begin to understand
Their talk of brokenness.

FROM ANNIGNONI'S 'JOSEPH' IN SAN LORENZO, FLORENCE

A plank
is a stairway
is a hammer
is a cross.

A man
is a treetrunk
is an artist
is a father, blessing.

The child
receives the sunlight
the scripture
the love.

For now the workshop is the world
is like a second skin to them both.

Where cloud intrudes,
it is flat, blood-red.

MOZART'S REQUIEM IN A VILLAGE CHURCH

There is some trepidation
In the rural strings
And more in the audience

As they shuffle in, cope
With pillars. Some, well-briefed,
Whisper of Süssmayr.

We begin. The bassoonist, punk, twenty,
Down from London by one-two-five,
Is easy with her part;

Her counterpoint is light –
She is not foxed by Bax
Or ruffled by Duruflé,

But as she plays I see
Her heart fall, Constanze's,
Into the scoring,

Our hearts, alto quavers,
Plaintive bird-cries,
Are overstridden in the bass –

We are all alone
With mortality
And the *Agnus Dei.*

At last the Requiem
Dies away into
Rook-broken quietness.

Punk and pensioner rest
A moment, at the lych-gate,
Brought together by a death.

MAGDALENE IN THE GARDEN

"If it is you, Sir, who have removed
him, tell me where you have laid him, and I'll
take him away. An end to this affair.
        Tell me where you have laid him.
Please. If only you will give him to me
we shall be alone together once –
there were always others, endless cares.
        Tell me where you have laid him.
And Judas always feared the chance of scandal –
as though there could be greater shame, than that
such a man should wring out his end, bared
        Tell me where you have laid him.
under Pilate's placard. John was wary too –
jealous, I'd say, though seeing him with Mary
yesterday – well – an end to envy's snare.
        Tell me where you have laid him.
Strange, we all thought more of each other yesterday,
weeping, waiting for soldiers to come,
remembering the freedom of the road, where
        Tell me where you have laid him.
we were so often hungry, dusty,
triumphant. Wondering if they'd move on Shabbat.
Those early days, you know, I did not dare
        Tell me where you have laid him.
look anywhere but his feet. A strong walker.
Loved the extra league, the tendons' stretch,
and I, too, loved it, beating out air,
        Tell me where you have laid him.
staying with him, though he'd always pick
out a slow one, strengthen up their stride,
I did not have him to myself, anywhere.
        Tell me where you have laid him.

How thoughts wander now – Shabbat on the road,
its unearthly peace, our lostness to all
but God – we'd nothing, but when he'd tear
        Tell me where you have laid him.
a loaf it was enough, it was life to us.
Tell me, and I, scorned for what I was, saved
by love alone, bitter as myrrh, will bear
        Tell me where you have laid him.
the cursed corpse away for last farewell,
asking the dead eyes guidance, giving
the dear mouth words… Why do you stare?
        Tell me where you have laid him.
Only give him to me, and I will drench
the dead feet with nard, and wipe them with my hair."

"Ma-ry."

PREACHING EASTER

Last meeting of the carers' group.
All were asked to bring
a symbol, an object to hold up
to show what the group
had *meant* to us.
Half had forgotten, but all,
dutifully, wrenched something
out of pocket or bag
and spoke on it.

Preachers, no less than the rest,
become wrenchers
of symbols, asserting things
of wood, wine, water and light
very near to lies

and all the time we
are wrenched by symbols
we shall never speak about –
those we almost managed to love,
and through the space of almost
have never understood, thinking
them wood, or wine,
water, or light –

those whom we have seen tear
the weft of life, doing it violence,
doing wrong we have colluded with
and fail to call
nails, or gall, or night.

Easter morning is the most outrageous
wrench of all, doing death violence,
ruining the space of almost.
It is as though God,
waiting his turn in the circle,
had given *his* answer,
dragging it up from somewhere –
some source of splinters, yeasts, floods,
and floods of light.

BIZARRE AT CHRISTMAS, 1992

for Anthony Burgess

[Burgess begins his novel *Earthly Powers* with the sentence: "It was the afternoon of my eighty-first birthday, and I was in bed with my catamite when Ali announced that the Archbishop had come to see me."]

It was the afternoon of the birthday
Of Jesus, and I was in bed
With my rain-giver when news
Was brought to me
Of bombs in bottle-banks
And boxes of chocolates,
And the murder, in a home,
Of a ninety-nine-year-old woman.

It was the afternoon of Jesus, and rains
Turned to snow in Sarajevo.
News was brought to me that
Little men in Transit vans
Were doing house-clearance
Behind the Bosnian refugees.

It was Jesus, somewhere
In the soaked, sticky,
Splintered, cloying,
Blasphemous old news.

III. LANDSCAPES

CLIMBING THE BEALACH MOR OF SUILVEN, SUTHERLAND

Last night's sunset
Turned the loch, and the stac behind
Bronze, brilliant,
The colour of the metal
On an axe-head, fresh from
Electrochemical cleaning.

Today the blue heron
Climbs across the loch. Grey seals slump.
We stumble up Suilven.
On reaching the ridge eyes
Weary of staring into the steep slope
Launch themselves off like eagles.

To Sutherland
I brought a mind rusty, afraid of keenness.
As I climb I feel the current mount –
Impurities electric-etched
Into the unchangeable hills.
I feel the ice-axe of my spirit

Slowly sharpen.

SYLLABLES

A house called Sand.
A farm called Fire and Smoke
from days of smugglers' signalling.
I walk the high woods around
these names – these codes for persisting.
Beech, larch and oak
are my texts, soft air my instruction.

An experiment in light –
to walk under a scraggy oak
is to see the sun
filtered, solvent-washed, bright–
glittering through a brilliant run
of beads. The larches soak
light away, a tighter, gloomier mesh.

An experiment in space –
from sleep above Sidbury I woke
thinking I was on an island
with earthworks its cliffs, a thin place
by heaven. Slowly the highland
vision, the blithe wild ease of it, broke;
Devon returned, all ridge and ditch and furrow.

Detail teaches. A stream-bed, now dry,
exposes the roots of an oak
on which in turn a thorn roots,
twists and forces its way
to light. Leaves, barbs, shoots,
all based on others' growth. A life's work
to read these ridges, lean true upon these trees.

This poem, and 'Building Materials', formed part of a commission from East Devon District Council.

THE BROWN HAWK

Still, on his dead oak stump, he sits, more
Like a Zen master than a brown hawk.

I long for him to fly, but
He is paradoxically idle, this symbol
Imperious. His government
Of the Empire is motionless.
In my garden I scrabble at thistle-roots.

At last he detaches himself, glides, turns,
Circles to a soar, studies the valley for game.

My eyes follow, I know
His natural history, his buzzardness,
Intimately, but
My boots sink into the soil;
I am no more hunter
Than a Zen master
Is the sound of the one hand.

REFLECTION AND TRANSMISSION

Fellows' Study, Hawthornden

the poet framed in sunlight
through a window.
in the mirror another window,
and through it beech-woods
singing of bud-burst
over the obbligato of the Esk in flood.

the doors are mirrors too,
reflect the books of past poets
transmitting in clear or not so clear.
the ceiling is a cave where thoughts settle,
conceal themselves,
the beams nestle closer to protect them.

sunlight – window –
window – mirror –
window in mirror in door.
sunlight in memory
on a lost lover's face
and the skin at her throat.

the poet says he is thinking of his work.
the trees try to get through to him.

BUILDING MATERIALS

Cottages on the Otter.
Cob of course –
a wonder, if the damp don't get in.
Chert stone, local. Thatch
from hand-threshed wheat.
Oak for beams and fittings.

'Twere all done proper, chances are,
'tween one Whit and the same Michaelmas.

And simple, seemingly, the make-up
of cottagers' lives
three hundred year ago.
No Concorde, or Internet,
VAT or CFC's.
Born, baptized, married, died,

all within a day's walk
in old boots.

What would we record of our brief lives?
Not mortgage rates, or GDP,
but who we loved, whether we spent time with them,
whether they forgave our petty treacheries;
if we had hope, and work to do,
or merely stone to break

to make
someone else's runway to heaven.

AN ARRIVAL OF HOUSE-MARTINS

Martins come to nest in the eaves.
Our three cats assemble, watch
from the window. They study a patch
of air criscrossed by dives
and by that quick stalling lifted
swoop with which creatures gifted
in the trick of flight attain their perch.
The cats spectate, search
with every ear-muscle
for a hint of weakness. The martins'
heads are like aimed dartings
of light, flashing out code for tussle
with numberless insects, childrens' hunger.
Three cats, their nemeses, linger.

TOTAL ECLIPSE OF THE SUN, CORNWALL, AUGUST 1999

Being ready means learning new language –
Chromosphere, Bailey's beads, the diamond ring;
The importance of getting to the zone of totality.

A triumph of Newtonian computation –
We can know to the moment
When to take off our safety-filters –
We are assured it is no mere spectacle
For mere observers such as we. Our sun is so bright
That this is one of the few chances for Science
To see it as it really is.

On the day, poised above Camborne, our safety-filters
Are like toddlers' toys discarded on Christmas afternoon.
Heavy cloud, intermittent rain, no beads, no ring;
Yet we do see something as it really is – rare enough
In these intertextual days.

We see the shadow of the moon roll heavy and unstoppable
In from the sea. The land, surprised, stutters and darkens.
Street-lights begin to strike. Squeals and streaks of flash-photography
Are offered up, but the darkness desires them not, rolls in, chill,
Not like night but only like itself.

Not like night, for far away to the south
Is the amber glow of continuing day,
But weighty reality hanging long enough
(The seagulls screeching, lifting for their clifftop homes)
To stir the most sceptical instinct.

Day comes back, as though at the roll of a dimmer switch.
There is an eerie gladness at the grey Cornish morning
Restored – no beads, no ring, but a strong contentment,
Beyond any dawn-song, that the sun should have come again.

The sun comes again, in veiled and thoughtful powers,
And sets, as specified in almanacs.
But none of us, that night, talks *Neighbours*,
Or ordinary things. The veil we cast
Over the reach and fear of living on this world

Was parted for seventy seconds of totality.
We return, from pilgrimage, enhanced
In things that go beyond the reach of words.

PROVENCE – LATE SUMMER

for Lydia and David

A place to lose track of days.
To rest eyes on fields
of sunflowers, faded, seed-heavy,
black as the richest soil.

To attend to the mistral's hiss
through the great plane tree in the courtyard
as warm gusts skid
the newly fallen leaves.

To dissolve imagination in
rivers – in the green
vibrant Isar,
turbulent with news of glaciers,

as it swirls into the Rhône and is lost
in the great slide past Avignon, past
the palace where Popes saw emissaries
from the Great Khan.

A maze of high cloud
filters pearl-like sunlight –
painter's light,
caressing colour out of nerve-ends.

And after any exertion
of gazing, or hearing,
or cleaning a brush,
to fortify the soul – velvet wine.

LATE NOVEMBER BUZZARDS

They stare me down, these mornings –
Each one darker than the last,
The oaks past their glory,
Dimming from rust to dun,
Inevitably to the purplish-grey of winter –
The buzzards stare me down, from telegraph poles,
Flight-feathers fluffed against the chill.

In more prosperous times they lift
At the car's coming, catching air
For the flat glide away from threat.
After a damp autumn, rabbits scarce,
Partridge chicks well hidden,
They grip their poles tighter,
Stare me sulkily down.

In more prosperous times I might stop, watch the lift,
Invest in the space to follow a glide,
A winding up invisible draughts towards the soar;
I might make poetry out of the precise flick
Of a narrowed wing at tree-height,
Making flight into art,
Rather than drudgery.

In these times of setting to another aging winter
I stare buzzards back,
And drive on,
And drive on.

WEST HIGHLAND SONNET

There is a sort of sadness, always, to these
glaciated landscapes. The hills lie scoured.
Recent ice, slow-dragged across corries
and cols, dumping debris thus devoured
on drab moraines, leaves a scarred sense,
weaves a slow traumatised song
much attacked by dissonance, dense
like late Beethoven, bleak, deaf-sung.

The Black Cuillins are the *Grosse Fuge* of the set –
strange, spiky, insistent to the edge of sanity
as to what *must* be – structure, at its limit,
shatters, leaving movement the only unity –
the theme, jagged, leaping, which redeems
a scoured sadness driven to extremes.

MATTERHORN FROM ZERMATT

Mont Blanc, from the Chamonix road,
Took up a quarter of the sky,
Seemed indeed a mountain made of sky.
Matterhorn – first sight – is rockness itself.

Merest feather of a cloud on the peak.
Other feathers gather from the west,
Harden into climbing hammers.

A mountain aloof
Complete in its own thoughts.
By starlight wraithlike.
By moonlight pale cream.

Up the path a million cameras
And some state-of-the-art gear
Amble with intent.

At the hotel
A woman from Ohio
Hates the coffee –
Worse even than Viennese –

A man from Peterhead
Finds Zermatt too full of Teriyaki
For his liking.

Below my window
An old man scythes a gentian-sprinkled meadow,
Planting the feet, keeping low,
A movement so practised as to flow without thought.

If I thought prayer
Easy for saints
I would think it was like this.

Last sight, after a storm.
Snow up to the Hörnli Hut,
Above that snow-coloured cloud.
Then, faint, the outline of the mountain,

At first like a shape laid into the weave
Of fine paper. Then bolder,
Every crevice clotted with cloud,
Every slab dusted with new snow.

IDENTIFYING WITH THE KURDS (1991)

for the refugees on the mountain passes in winter

Step on step
At every step stones slip back
Strike soles dragged
Into the shifting slope
And dragged on
Into steeper shale
And air like sharper flint.
Some of them carry young children.

I had dragged feet
Up narrow paths,
Stronger walkers behind.
I had suffered on the Glyders,
Stumbled on High Stile.
I had lusted for mountain air.
Some of them have no shoes.

In Scotland, next summer,
I'll try once more
To keep my day-bag light;
I'll fight off vertigo,
Count off a Munro,
Point out the car
Far below.
Some of them rip up the heart.

I'll stumble,
Aim my eyes
Into shifting stone,
See
Briefly
Kurdistan.

ROSETTA

from the flooding in Mozambique in early 2000. Media pictures included a woman who had given birth to her baby in a tree

We lost sight of Sophia
In some parking-lot or other;
The wisdom to plan for the next generation
Deserted us – or we abandoned her
For reminding us
Of free-market failure.

To attract our attention
Sophia has to lie sprawled in a tree
While the stream she was born by
Hurls below her,
Swollen, twisting,
Junk-strewn, body-strewn.

In her moment in the news
Sophia gives birth – not to the anointed one
But to one more peasant baby for the millennium -
Rosetta. Born in a tree.
Fragility among thorns.
Daughter of wisdom.

Let it not take three thousand years
For us to decipher her.

YOSEMITE VALLEY

I. From Washburn Point

Mile and mile and mile of pines,
the ground hidden, always rising.
Finally a vista which,
so much looked for, appals.
The glacier-track is a sick gleam
of exposed, raked rock,
like work still in the studio
of some macabre sculptor.
I have longed to see this
and now want to declare it
unfinished, not yet ready
for its public, till trees are born
on the scars, and the cliff faces
heal.

II. From the Merced River

The valley is a tunnel of lighting effects:
ivories on Half-Dome, while other
cliffs, Eumenides, wait
in grave-grey silence
to have their say.
On mountain faces
the strivings of unproved braves
climbing amid the weaving swifts,
and old profiles, like Titian's
self-portrait at ninety.
Evening comes, and morning,
and these hills are there to be sought,
to change me, as they themselves
change.

III. Retrospect

A way-station of the imagination
between the High Sierra
and the sea. A snapshot
of rock-cutting fate. And if
it be true, and I believe it,
Nature sings of her creator,
Yosemite then's a cradle
of this praise.

IV. PROMISING THE MOON IN HELL

PROMISING THE MOON IN HELL

There must be a minor circle of hell, I think,
where the occupants, free from boiling pitch
or sulphur, unprodded with pitchforks,
distant from Satan's icy rage,
are immersed instead in grant applications.

Fifty copies must be sent. In each
the applicant must promise
that in the course of the project
speeding locomotives will be overtaken,
work of peerless genius brought to birth.

The great and the good must appear as referees
(not, in hell, such a problem to contact them).
The perfect padded envelope must be found
at the bottom of a vast basket
of similar envelopes. No material

of any human interest may be enclosed.
At terminals and desk-top publishing packages
they sit, their crime on earth
too much unregenerate desire
to set their mark upon the world

as poets, scholars, persons of letters.
And every form comes back the same:
Application Excellent. Funding Denied.
Fifty copies must be sent. In each
the applicant must promise...

ASH – SIX POEMS FOR A BORROWED ALSATIAN PUPPY

1. Early Morning Walk

First mists of sunrise.
I struggle with the gate into the top field -
you have already surged your puppy mind
through it (having whined and wriggled
round and under)
                    go headlong for the slope.

Exercising forethought,
I wonder if one of those shapes
on the ridge is a bull.
You saw your first cow
yesterday, cannot be expected to know.

You do not look back
to the vast view of morning,
oak-crowns through the mist,
the gift of morning. You yank me on
beyond fog and forethought.

2. Ball Under Chair

Ball under chair
stretch a nose
stretch a paw
bark at it
stalk it –
pretend to ignore it
try another toy
finally
seek help.
Much the way I came
to prayer.

3. Asleep

Asleep. A bundle of paws
fat and tawny like those of lions.
Ears twitching faintly,
Ash sleeps the sleep of the young
gathering their strength.
His head is heavy with learning:
a first greenfinch,
smell of our river.

As I watch
stomach and rump begin to shiver,
dreams set in;

pose changes. The head thrust forwards,
paws back, gathered in pairs,
imitating a caveman's antelope
or a heraldic supporter
asleep at his post.

4. Even Earlier Walk

At this appalling hour,
light only barely lifting
mist pockets off hedges,
I notice secrets
(wrestling with frozen binder twine):
a fox pursuing his purposes
past a line of statue cattle,
a buzzard, low, incessant,
far mew from his noonday soaring,
scours the rabbit graze.

Not so secretly the same three coal tits
as every morning
start from the same thorn bush;
you point ears at them
as though they had just been created
without your approval.

Three plunging fields later
we straggle back
into the first sun
which studs dewed leaves with brilliancy
and one of us is tired.

5. Haiku

Rain. The stinging, blind
soak of it. Rain, the one thing
puppies don't notice.

6. Memories of Ash

Your bark – three times the weight of you.
The things you chewed.
Your wearisome jealousy, whining
at the least hug we gave each other.
The depths of your puppy-sleep after a good walk.

Most of all one leap
at a stick hurled
twenty feet above you.

It cartwheeled into the wet hillside;
you shoulder-plunged after it
as dogs do. But first you jumped
your whole body following its line of flight
weightless of care or calculation:

joy can be.

BOYS AT PLAY

Aside in a letter from Bertrand Russell
to Ottoline Morrell. 'Wittgenstein
very argumentative and tiresome.
He simply would not concede
that it was impossible
that there was a rhinoceros in the room.'

A logic tussle of two supple minds. History
has tended to favour Russell. Ponderous
hooved mammals, gazing sullenly,
prehistorically, over lowered horns,
are largely absent from photographs
of the Cambridge of the time.

Wittgenstein at Linz,
in the days of the old Empire,
was briefly at school with Hitler –
the rich Jew-boy with the world's
great hater. Both loved art,
and *Meistersinger.*

Russell never saw a sullen eye
take on the crazed stare
that precedes the charge. Wittgenstein
had seen, knew better than Bertie
the animals that live around boys at play:
the rhino, the cur, the Wagner-loving jay.

THE FALL

They'd been there for years, of course,
Hugging trees, logging the animals by name,
Taking afternoon tea with the Lord God -
Occasionally He would stay for spritzers.

They were pretty cool, those gatherings
In the cool of the day,
But well, you know, things happen.

One day when Adam was classifying arachnids
Eve began to coil her imagination around a certain serpent -
Virtual, of course, but so green
It made the green mamba look pale,

So sinuous it made her screen blur before her eyes
And you can guess the rest.

She went ahead and clicked on a new icon –
It was the one on which God had said
She shouldst on no account click.

At once she was offered
A free holiday. She called Adam over
And they interfaced as never before.

Then they looked at each other, and knew
That what they'd been doing till then
Was not just living, as they'd thought.
It had been *a lifestyle choice.*

All too short a step from there
To making bad ones.

V. THE SOUL'S TUNIC

THE REUNION

We assemble, in the long library,
The scent in the beeswax of the polish
Of which is precisely unchanged, and
Exchange, over dinner, surfaces,
Contrasted marriages and careers;
While we are sober we do not look
Too near the grain
For fear of harsher weathering.

The solicitors have worn dark and safe, their secrets
Locked in boxes lettered white on black.
The bankers have taken a high veneer;
They bellow bond-issues at each other,
Point out honours on boards,
Put down sons on ten-year plans.
The doctors' eyes have seen fifteen years'
Pain, and have not come to discuss it.

I recognise only the face of the engraver,
The gouger of glowing copper. There
I see ravages – seams of work worn out,
New workings, going deeper
For deeper ore.
His work has taught him time –
The shortness of it, the disciplined
Desperation of working in a corroding
Medium, with hands that will not
Always be steady, the challenge of the virgin
Surface, so easily sinned on.

We are drunk now, flushed
With the wine that used to be forbidden.
We talk, arthritis, debt,
And thirty-year sentences –
Terms of mediocrity.
We are etched, all of us,
Unvirgin, imprecise alloys,
By the royal acid of the will of God.

But for Morning Chapel,
Tomorrow, at eleven,
Our masks will be safely on.

BEARING REALITY – FOR SILKE BISCHOF

Silke Bischof was taken hostage by bank-robbers in August 1988, and appeared in numerous (posed) pictures in the media. She was shot during a police ambush. She was 18.

Step out of role, Silke, don't you go
Playing with men with big guns again.
We cannot bear much of you and him –
Not with our breakfast things – cereal
Just does not go with undiluted
Fear. We would like to be directors –
Call for a cut and hand you cashmere
Sweaters and smiles, and say no more takes
Like that one, Silke dear, you were just
Brilliant. Eyes held the right stillness –
Death in them. I liked the hair, which you
Couldn't brush back – Dieter's gun hand stopped you
(Only his thumb on the hammer kept
You alive – very good, that last touch) –
Your lower lip starting to go forward,
Sobs coming but for now unstated.
Cut of near genius, we'd tell each other,
Safe in the canteen, and you'd smile and shrug.

You are a still, Silke, unsmiling.
We will see gun hand and eyes, lips,
Fair, girlish hair for a long long time
After we throw the newspaper out.
We'll all the while yearn to run the film
On, to find somewhere in your last hours
Quality, richness of life, even
God perhaps. Nothing presents itself.
No smile. Not even the arched-shouldered
Scream behind that look of steady fear.
Press work gets better and better of course –
Shot good of Dieter, binoculars,
Leather and hammer-clawing hand –

Photographer got all that, and you did not
Turn your head once – at the ambush made
Just enough space to be shot in the heart,
Leaving us that quite still, lovely,
Aspirationless face, remembered

Long past your name, and our
Thousandth debate about evil.

INCARNATION

The beach at dawn.
Early pelicans – seven –
Sweep the sea, fishing.
Still-invisible sun seems to glow
On their backs. Again they beat the sea,
Big-winged, taking, then pass on.

Where the early light
Touches the water
There is promise.
Elsewhere dark –
Steel-dark, steel-blue-dark
As of a peregrine's back.

You know birds and stars, know
What it is to look from a high mountain.
The sand beneath your feet is gritty.
The clean moments pass.
The cold drains blood from your hands.
You can be confident only of sunrise.

At the other end of the beach the disciples huddle,
Knowing you are praying.

THANKSGIVING, RURAL NORTH CAROLINA

The light sepia, from a low, reflected sun.
Three women, old, standing under a tree
By a low white frame house
Photographed in farewell.

They are still as the photographs
They will pore over when we are gone,
Still as the old oak, whose shadows
They know by heart.

Another Thanksgiving. A baby – five years since the last –
Fifteen since Will put a hunting rifle in his mouth
After the turkey, and the dressing,
And the collard greens, and the water-melon-rind pickle.

The aunts give gifts, fuss over the child,
Seeing dimly, remembering the rifle.
Later we, looking over the sights of cameras,
Ready ourselves to remember them.

Forty years on, Star Wars permitting,
We'll be dim-sighted seers
Patient, with gifts, in blurring shadows;
We'll have our stories –

'Yes, I knew Great-Grandmother, and Ruth, and Viola.
They were...' courage, and blind kindness –
Our icons, grown now to oak-roots
And palm-fronds.

SUNSET OVER EXMOOR

From the Crown Hotel, Exford,
Where they still have stabling for gentlemen,
We watch the sunset by dint
Of discount vouchers. There almost had
To be a poem there, to justify the bill.
Privilege. Poetry at several pounds a line.

Is it accountability, then,
That draws from me
How those clouds lie
On that western hill
Like quill pens,
Their feather-edges honed
As the sun falls away from them,
Gone to boil the sea beyond Lynmouth?

Or is it love
That gives me eyes and words?
The deer think their way
Up onto the hill, beside the sky,
That same love's
Most generous calligraphy.

SESTINA FOR KAREN AND ROS AND SUE, RICHARD AND PETER AND SIMON, AND MANY OTHERS

I came here when I was nineteen, to get well
from a kind of flash-flood of down, from a tyrant rule
of spiders over the thin moon of me. Safe from harm
here, they said. The film'll run slowly. Under control.
No-one will have to know. No-one will notice.
They didn't say I'd come out with a label.

Mind you, it was a kind of comfort, the label,
at first. People could see I'd fallen down a well
that was real. It made them take notice.
Then we lost our insurance. It's a rule,
the girl on the phone said. So I lost control
and broke the phone. My friend left. Only then the self-harm

and the Seclusion Room. What's the harm,
I said, if I cut myself? Is that the wrong label?
They tried things out till I was under control:
thirty milligrams the spiders. Seventy milligrams, well,
numbness, like living yesterday over. Fifty mgs rule
O.K. Not disruptive enough to notice.

I watch the trees a lot. I stand by the notice
that says all visitors must sign in and out. Harm-
less words. I tell another patient it's a good rule.
He tells me I'm a police spy. I like that label.
Whoever made my loneliness made it well.
But who was it? And is he still in control?

Sometimes I stand and think—this is a sick plan to control
a special person who's been fighting stuff a long time. 'Notice
the difference, when you treat me right!' I shout. Does no harm.
It *is* better here, than years ago. Same label –
but they ask about the colour of the bricks in your well.
Sometimes they help you choose to go ahead and keep a rule.

Maybe it has to be that certain drugs rule
your life, that without them there's just no control
over the downs. But staff *do* talk to you, go past the label,
if you get the right one, with some time to notice
you. To see you're choosing between living and no more harm
ever again. I read once that all shall be well–

tell me then: if I knew every rule, and could get people to notice
me, and was under control with the drugs, and was no harm
to anyone, and lost my label, would I be called well?

commissioned by the local NHS Trust to express the concerns of long-term sufferers of mental illness, and read in the Service held in Exeter Cathedral to mark 50 years of the NHS in Devon.

POEM FOR THE MILLENNIUM

commissioned by Holy Trinity Church, Drewsteignton, as part of the celebrations of the two thousandth year since the birth of Christ

The Queen, the Archbishop and the Blairs
watch samba in a stretch-tent.
We wait out the old era
in the Church, in the Drewe,
by the woodstove. We wake to 2000
curious to see and to be, to ring in the new
but

the Fingle Brook still sucks at the same
stubborn tree-roots, still swings the main channel of the Teign
only fractionally from its line, still loses itself
in the stream, scarps of quiet woodland watching.

The same buzzard hunches, cloak-feathered,
on the same telegraph pole, stares down
the rain, anatomising frosted mud.
Drenched and furtive rabbits fuel his frown.

The same chill air scuffs the face
of the Church, testing for weakness,
draws the collars of walkers and worshippers
tighter. Christ promised the world to meekness
but

the same arbitrary sunlight still seems to split
some raindrops to prisms, elicit from others
only monochrome. Where then the turning,
where life's new, transfigured colours?

We enter a century where fresh water will be precious,
and farming has already grown hard. Humans are very many
now. We over-stuff our atmosphere
with greenhouse gas, and tweak at genes.
The snowdrops come earlier, storms blustrier.

John Tavener in the stretch-tent. The singers are young –
their yearning, hugely disciplined, floats
high, hints at more than itself,
drifts like brilliantly-lit dust-motes
beyond fear of the Bug, hype of the Dome.

Let there be respect for the travestied Earth,
peace that is more than mock-process,
love that seeketh not its own.
Let there be delight – old-fashioned word, closest
we can come to naming joy.
Let there be forgiveness, a new start.

That night, over Dartmoor,
the sky is crystalline with the point-fires of stars,
like gifts from light-millennia away.

Let gift of hope transfigure
this Devon ridge, these Iron Age
memory-banks.

Let there be possibility here for turning

Let us catch hints of the sort of love
humans have rarely ever tried.
A love, that, transcending death in earth,
is hinted at, could we but grasp it,
in the shadowed brook, and in ember-light,
and floods the blustery air.

COBALT THERAPY AGAIN TODAY

Cobalt therapy again today,
After the diagnostic technetate.
Shares in isotopes rise –
Her red count drops.
Her hair falls out – it
Was expected.

Nothing is expected of the treatment;
These are secondaries. She stays,
Too cheerful to bear for long,
With the priest.
She would have liked
To have seen a healer,

But this is resisted.
Gamma sources must have their turn.
Only when those fail
Will they re-label her,
Give her the glamour and nepenthe
Of terminal care.

On retreat, in the sandstone light
Of a Saxon chapel, we pray for her,
Taking the roof off our lives –
Letting her down inside us.
The intensity shocks.
We tremble as the rays hit.

Who then is holding whom
On the stretcher?
The door swings open
Between light and light.
We cannot look. She is too weak
To unfasten her shoes.

The many doors
Of our castles
Swing open in sympathy.
We are irradiated, room by room,
Our favourite cankers
Targets now.

We would rather have had the drugs.
We long for her to dance again.
We long for death, to take away the weight of glory.

SLIPCATCHERS

Jane is ill enough now to be firmly labelled
Dying. We speak the forbidden word, but
Living would be more accurate
For every day has a different quality.

There are two boys. At their age
I fielded slip for a school eleven –
An alarming promotion. The space
Of possibility seemed vast, my arms leaden.

Now I am part of the care team
Who chatter at Jane, keeping up
Our spirits, and break off
To prognosticate for God.

We talk little now of healing.
The future is narrow-waisted,
We begin to look
Past the constriction.

The boys become our focus, and we
Unwilling slipcatchers
Poised in a cordon, waiting for them
To fly from the involuntary edge,

Uncertain if the deflection
Will be fine and fast, or slow, looping,
The grief hard to sight
Against the light
Of the forbidden city.

CROWS AT A FUNERAL

Wheeling under laden, pall-coloured cloud
The carrion birds. Seeing them yaw and pitch
And corkscrew across the storm, the day we all
Went to bury Helen, I could not help
Admire persistence in the *Corvidae.*

They're up in all conditions, and though
We scan the sky for more uplifting symbols
The crows are compulsory. Fair-weather
Soaring hawks, planing ease, are like
The life of adverts for Pernod and jeans –

Lazy, effortless, taloned, and rapacious.
These black banalities mob our soarings,
Turning too quickly outside our grasp,
Slipping away from reprisal, raucously calling
'Decay, decay, and death that gives us life'.

This teeming day, full of tears and weather,
Holds little for hedonists. A caucus of crows
Blusters through our consciousness. We talk
Raucously of resurrections. The certainty
Is deposited in the over-full churchyard.

Our hope, beyond the bitter wind, is in
The Word that made the ravens, arrayed lilies,
Cast crows as reality. Who suffered
To make sense for us of loss, and service,
And of this so sullen, leering, anvil sky.

HOLLY LEAF

for Sandy

You find for me a holly leaf, last year's,
Reduced by time to a fine skein, an outline
In brittle thread of what had shone with green
Last June. So it is with my faith too, although
I do not show such doubt, but promise you
An Incarnation-poem from the leaf
That sits so obstinate upon my desk.

I do not know if it is nurture, patience,
Or His long, terrifying suffering of us
That lets elaborate construct fade,
Unseenness stay, as we think on God.
In China they are rounding up the free –
Their future suddenly brittle, faded.

And so I write about a thing which, mainly
Space and silence, still retains the outline
Of a tiny crown of thorns, and whispers too
Of Christmas. Holly we believe
Is evergreen, and evil not as strong
As good. Counter-example tears the weft –
But what persists is fine, beyond evaluing.

KINDS OF FAITH

You ask – if I can see the green
In this long swoop of fields

Down off the moor, as we pick our way
By moonlight. I say we can't – I say

We infer the colour, that that is part
Of the beauty. What stretches the heart

Has in fact the hue of settled snow.
But you say, having waited, and heard, no:

We *can* be definite – though the dance
Of space, hedged, arranged, is at the last

Limit of our sense, the retina
Retains the green. The shared blear

Of snowlight sweeps to the scarp's edge.
We can agree, at least, that glory follows death.

FUNERAL FILMS

"to understand bereavement
we must first come to terms
with our own deaths."
from a training session on death & dying

I have a clear picture of my own
Funeral. Threatened rain has held off;
The light is limpid, photographic,
The church four-square, full, every pew
Taken, but the churchwardens cope.

The sermon is brief and to the point.
A cello suite is played without flaw.
There are many tributes, even from
Those I hardly knew, and mourners
Weep decorously at the graveside.

My film of *her* service is blurred–
I know that short, brisk, Crem. formula,
But I do not hear it, or notice
When it ends. My life's shutter is jammed.
Anger churns inside me, anger at her –
I would rather stay angry than
Be alone. I taste that death's dry swallowing
And seize hold of the anger;
Endlessly I play it back at God –
I cannot see, I cannot see why

There will not always be this cleanness,
This brilliance of late breakfasts, coffee
Smells, and Scarlatti, and oranges,
And Lapsang-coloured shadows on silk,
And port-coloured shadows
In evenings of light remembering.
Instead bedpans, vomiting, incontinence,
Sedations, sad layings-on of hands,
Instructions unheard, incoherent,
The sudden nearness of God, and dark.

And so when the session is over
I fix up tennis, plan holidays
For the year after next, hold her
Tighter than need be. I leave both films
To fog in the light of prayer. As Saint Teresa
Says, we must open every door
In the mansion, and let love in.

I pray
To be the one left. I pray
Never to be left.

PALIMPSEST – A PRAYER

I have been in your in-tray all my life
Though I did not know it
And thought I wrote
My own itinerary
In my own alphabet
On the rough, second-grade vellum
You had provided.

I cannot read those old destinations
Now – nor have I love enough
To regret them. I can only peer
Into the bare, summary logia
Running from future to past across
My much-corrupted palimpsest.
Your Aramaic style is good, although
They say you could not write,
And knew no Greek,
And told good stories,
Lived and died them.

Hold up the parchment, Lord,
Scrape the surface clean.
It is scored through and through
With failed love for virtue,
Obscuring the Kingdom's character-set.
Inscribe me a song to sing –
And give me the prodigal's part;
I know by heart the song
Of the other brother.

Write in light, Lord,
That I may still read
When my blood cools,
Still remember
When my song fails,
Still catch sight of you

When I sit to write,
Or share
In breaking bread.

THE MOSAICIST

When I was younger I would sometimes boast
In gold, and calculate a grand design.
Now I know I lack that taint, the almost-
Madness of creation, the genius of line.
I colour others' angels, attempt again
The sturdy Tree of Life – consistency
Of halo, hart, and heav'n, technique leaf-thin,
In these must be my petty mastery.
And they have made me teacher now, among
The shining stones, discerner of early talents;
My self-denial, the smile I give the young
As mists of colour stir, is read as balance.
The Lord alone knows patience for a liar
And how I long to see these dusts take fire.

LEANING ON THE SPRING – A PRAYER

Leaning out along a beech-branch
High above a quick-flowing river
I watch the buds mottle and fatten
Towards leaf-point
And spread my weight out
For what seems like the first time in years,
Spread out my weight onto the gathering spring.

For years now hope
Has been quickly followed by disaster
And I have learned to furl it close.

Uncurl it, Lord, this Eastertide –
I know the water's transience
And yet the sunlight makes on it
A standing jigsaw
Bright as filigreed silver.
I know the hurt of many memories
And yet when swimming collies
Shatter the bright pattern of the Esk
My doubting will gladdens,
My knotted heart stretches towards healing.

Unfurl, I pray, my trust again.

THE HOLED STONE

Like a displaced moonstone it lies
Holed rim canted to the sky, letting light through,
Mute, like a terrorist's victim
Holding up a maimed limb in silent complaint.

Usually I show off the Holed Stone
In sunlight, the luminous
Wounded rock after the stone circle
And the lonely clapper (which is like

A tombstone, yet from which
The Wallabrook, flashing
Oil colours off the moor-light,
Rushes into the young Teign).

To climb the Down today was to walk
Into a wall of wind. Not to notice
The rain for blasting, battering,
Until jeans stuck themselves to skin.

I stood on that down as on an Atlantic
Breaker, or a savage Scottish rock-peak,
Dead-reckoned, tacked,
Struck out southwards for the Holed Stone.

Battered, canted, benighted moonstone
Glistened out of the dusk,
In the sleeting, vicious Earth-rain,
Like a vision, above the white rage of stream.

On the bank in the darkness I paused.
The leap was foolish, too far,
Too far, how stupid I would look, stuck
In that torrent. I should go home, curl up with tea.

Still the Stone pulled me.
It was not living, just to turn back,
The flood racing by, the wind coaxing, not enough
To show this off in sunshine.

At last, shaking, I stood on the stone,
A waterproofed huddle hiding
The hideous entry-wound.
I looked upriver, into the storm's face.

Holding cagoule-cords in my teeth,
Drawing the shelter flat across my cheeks, leaving
A narrow crescent of vision
Below the soaked wool of a pudding hat,

I stared at the Teign. A flood
Such as would move mountains, or pierce
Vulnerable, passive plates of granite,
Surged towards and under me. Raw-eyed I looked away.

Below the wound in the stone the water was dark
As Acheron, or Styx. Yet even as I hid
The wind beat and beat on me
Till I was its creature. I have longed
To live my life in such passionate state
Vision narrowed on God,
Inhaling the raging of his Spirit,
The *ruach elohenu*, but mainly huddle,
Fearful, shocked by it, staring into
The wound God made in himself, letting love through,
His great symbol, eloquent, empty, canted to eternity.

Note : *ruach elohenu* (Hebrew) – the Spirit of our God

VI. BEYOND THE BITTER WIND

BEYOND THE BITTER WIND

It was on a certain night
when a certain moon
told Prospero it was the time;

this moon to the naked eye full
brilliant white – eliciting from every
reflecting surface on the whole island
silver.

A disc of cloud, cream, amber, as backdrop.
Above the disc
a million fine streams of paler cloud
fashioned in the lunar crucible
streamed away beyond the range of light.
Miranda grown, and come into her power.

Yasser Arafat, that old sticker, fathers
a child of hope, Yahnua,
conceived in Gaza
but born in Paris (the peace process
not so far advanced as to guarantee
freedom from the infections of the gutter).

Such moments lead to dreams –
the child, Moslem father, Christian mother,
growing up to have
a Jewish husband.
Gaza knowing justice,
Jerusalem *shalom*.
Fancies. Gaza's sewage
cries out from the ground.

Blown gulls over a steep hillside
glitter in sunlight in a way
leafless trees cannot catch.
The trees, stolid, swallow the earth's sap,
root the soil,
feed gulls their oxygen.
Neither the respiration cycle
nor the turn of gull-wing in light
is Ariel, yet each is a mark
of his industrious playfulness.

You might catch sight of him
in the bronze-red flickering
of a kestrel's wing, the bird
a dozen different balances
on the air's energy;

in the glitter of raindrops
studding the leaves of a Japanese maple,
their sudden showering
at a chance breeze;

or by the swarm of honeysuckle
up an ancient sandstone wall –
scent out of a field
of rusty sunlight –
Ariel and all his quality.

Discern, with spectroscopes,
signs out of signs.

When the crops fail,
and the women are raped
as military policy,
we end on the ground wondering
who we can best curse.

The dust groans.
The dust groans, being found as human flesh
peeling, shard-scratched. The wind keens.
On a cairn we add to
for reasons
we have forgotten
the elders sit.
There is said to be aid
at the camps to the east.

Ariel shows himself, laughingly,
in the highlights of a hillside
after new snow, in the slip of light
across an ice-sheet.
He entertains himself
arraying frost on bracken
making bridges of icicles;
then has to find for Prospero
the raw materials for snowshoes.

Blizzards are a favourite way
to wriggle inside his serfdom.
They show artistry, can blow
several ways at once, some flakes
seeming weightless, others streaming
downwind like deer fleeing a lion.
Skipping on each one in turn
he can still say it was
statistical fluctuation,
as his master's cars straggle
an abandoned freeway.

Among his quality, winners of his races,
ichneumon wasps
parasitic on caterpillars, their larvae
paralysing their hosts,
eating them alive from the inside.
Mimesis of fear itself.

Fear is among the engines
Ariel sets to work,
when the sun first breaks winter's hold
and casts the shadows
of what will be spring.
Fear of dying unreproduced;
archaic fear of leopard
at the waterfall.

Closest to his nature
is the energy that snaps
leathers of bud
and roars across the slopes
that birth *must* be given.

We, the Ferdinands of the developed West,
have the luxury of controlling our fertility,
questioning our identity –
conjuring Mirandas at will,
selecting them
off the satellite channels.

We have the possibility
of buying bottled water
scented with the scent of synthetic
apricots, of projecting yields
of futures
almost to the end of the decade.

We have the necessity of fears
which, while they do not manage
to drive the Dow-Jones down,
still give rise to the feeling
that we must do more research
into impending catastrophe.

Over the hills the Nazarene came
singing and healing the sick;
they were there to meet him, always,
to tear at his heart
and draw lots for his company.

The sea-horse and the coral reef,
the starfish and the shark.

It is of the nature of young love
to believe itself original –
never did such brilliant princeness
strut by such a pure constant
waterfall. Never were crescendi
so exquisite. For such moments
Ferdinand labours.
Sixty grand a year and a double plot
on the South Side
are Prospero's stipulation.

Miranda, over the years,
sits in Chinese silk
in ostrich feathers
in earrings of anodised titanium.

Ariel, night and day,
casting and weaving,
generates this finery.

Counselled by Caliban:
'do ye but steal his books..

Remember how Sycorax, my mother,
would dance, red hair flailing,
how the whole island danced.
Think how Prospero's power spread
like ink across a page.
Not a branch stirred willingly –
only to your misplaced coercion,
much-deceived air-sprite.

Bow down instead at Sycorax' tomb
pray if you must, but see you
steal his books..

be swift now – for the whole island's sake –
crash his files.

He made the light of this place

(which had jinxed about the headlands,
made bowls of fool's gold out of the bay
and haloed the clouds at sunset
with fantastical dragons)

take up the angles
of a Renaissance cloister,
then of mill-chimneys
piercing the line of a steep Pennine valley.
Then of factory-gates,
the people, reduced to sticks, queuing;
finally the reactor dome's
clean, remote curve.

He burned by means of a lens
of beaten silver
the thickets where he knew
I liked to hide

and you, tame spirit,
danced on every photon.

Do penance now, for Bhopal, Cernobyl -
if you can –
but fight back.'

An awkward script. Penance
is so old-fashioned.
We would rather hear of the young Miranda:
how she needed her sleep, but woke
face shining at the glory of day;
how she believed in people, knowing few,
could not imagine that mere systems
might stand in the way of goodness.
She loved Snoopy, and Pooh Bear, and Kierkegaard,
thought the moon overrated.
She danced into womanhood
sure-footed on spiders' webs
having not yet learned to look down
into the tearing weft.
Save her father
                    her heart was for none but Ariel
for the way he kept her eyes high
searching corries for eagles,
thunderstorms for rainbows.

She loved the douce and tricksy web he spun her mind
hated the demanding desire of others –
the kisses they insisted on
in car-parks –
but learned their struggle,
learned, in twenty years,
that Prospero's magic
leaves the air thin at the edges;
even Prozac
cannot mend the skein.

Skin stretched taut – not across
the flat curves of a supermodel's tan
after expensive aerobic tuning –
but across a friend's scalp,
across his cold hands.
A cancer thrives, the drugs
chase it up and down the spine.
Hope blurs, and goes.
He is in a territory far from her,
knows it well, tolerates
her terrified bridge-building
as the eyes of an old African refugee
might tolerate a TV crew.

the children wait at the door
the parent stares at the fire
the smallest choice is too heavy

the children wait at the door
the parent stares at the fire
broken gossamer curls upon itself,
attracts dust, drifts, dust-strewn.

We only snap our magic staves
and give ourselves to prayer
when the frame breaks
by which we circumscribed the world
our private isle...

the crucibles we'd thought perfect
and sequestered for lifelong magic,
used to fuse the scents of our emotion,
show flaws and crack. Mercury trickles out,
grey-eyed tears trickle, merge.
We had not thought projections so corrosive..
we had not thought..

Bartimaeus by the roadside blind
ready with his Messianic words.
Affirm the healer, make him feel
good about himself.
Take what you can get.

The sea-horse and the coral reef.
the starfish and the shark.

The Speech of Job's wife

They give me one verse
out of forty-two chapters in all.
Oh, and I come in briefly
when my husband is afraid
his breath might smell.
As though I could care
could summon enough sense of myself
to kiss anyone
or be kissed.

The news from Uz lacks enchantment.
There was a man, my husband,
of whose fortitude in the face of trials
are written the forty-two chapters
aforesaid, of Holy Writ.
But even that chronicle
of how he suffered and disputed
with the creator of all our woes
lines a coffin with taffeta,
paints with gold leaf
the surface
of a sewage pipe.

To articulate words you know are heard
is a richness.
To stay silent for a week
counts as wisdom
if anyone would have heard
what you left unsaid.

Behind the sound-bites you get in the Book
is the grind
the unfreedom
of never enough food,
not being able to think for sores.
When your sense of wonder
contracts to watching your arms
and wondering where the bloodsucking
will start next – landing so lightly
as the tsetse do. Leaving gorged
unless you're quick. Which by the end
of a day lugging firewood I'm not.

I do not find my voice in the sacred text,
What press I do get is bad
though I kept him going on gruel
through all those clever flights of repartee
most of which I'd heard before.
The worst of it was: knowing I was right –
knowing that I'd judged to a micron
how it would be.
That the only recourse from the torment
slogging for wood
nursing the fire
gruel
sleep
knowing one's mind going
was to take leave of God.
Knew it to a micron. *He*
was simply wrong.

There are waters that cure
and waters only to weep by.
There are pallets taken up
by those set free to walk,
pallets covered with suppurations
burned after a death. And madness
burns, at our convenient explanations.

The sea-horse and the coral reef,
the starfish and the shark.
And Lazarus, dragged blinking from the tomb.

The woman who anointed Jesus

It was a chill spring. The men
came in wanting their wine hot
and fast comfort. You
waiting on them,
accepting the wine's bite –
they poured it into or sometimes over you –
turning to the fire for refuge.

That night you stepped practically into his arms
he smelled of sheep, remember?
You of tangy smoke and rough wine
and self-pity.
He went from there to the Pharisee's house
and you were there crying and kissing his feet
and wasting the hookers' nard
on the first man you'd ever trusted.

I poured death on the life-giver, yes.
He said he approved, said
it was good to get the taste of it
while it could still run off him
dripping onto the flagstones
like honey off a board for making bread

I rubbed death into his feet with my hair
oh, the tingle of death, so close to me.

Riddles

How can a gale blow in a library
without disturbing the classification?
Sweep away the whispered nuance
to leave the lust
                                        the longing by the waterfall
for the tablet of ecstasy?

How can a face, jarred by words, rain sorrow
as though from an inner glacier
never exhausted – the same tear-tracks
even when there is no crying –
the same shriek, unheard, for relief?

Question

        Dunblane.
Thomas Hamilton.
        Turned his gun on a school.
        What words were said at his funeral?
Who went?

I will go up into the wind again –
set myself into the blasting wind
to be blown like the
cottongrass
and the logan-stone;
I will set my face to go up
into the whirlwind.

Always the bitter wind,
repeating the music of chaos,
beating round the enchanted isle
where even magicians cannot stay,
whipping at the soil of Uz.

It blasts the angles of faith,
shaves the stone of temples.

It blows the Lord up to Jerusalem.

Prospero, in Milan, aged away at once
to gold-gowned dust.
                                        Under the bridge at Charing Cross
it blows too cold for snow.

Strife is loose upon the wind;
they change the guard in the praetorium.

A new governance promises much;
the Empire is itself.

Only.. a donkey climbs a hill.

Resist the unrolled scroll
                          Hand it back to the attendant.
Are not Abana and Pharpar
                          rivers of Damascus
equally proud, lucid, ambivalent streams?

Torchlight. Cold slicing through cloaks.
The last act of a zealot's dream.
Inevitable pundits not quite excluded
from the high priest's house
foment fragments of news.

The smell of his tunic, his hands' curve
in blessing bread,
touch of them washing feet,
are all you have.

You shall be called Peter
You shall be called Peter-who-warmed-himself-at-the-brazier
the cold of that night
slowing thought
slowing the blood in fingertips, slowing thought
across the courtyard

to stand there at all
your declaration of love
face in shadow
edge on to the expediency
that one man die for the people.

What was truth that week?
Given into the puzzling eyes of women –
into the anointing hands at Bethany,
the quiet maidservant
in the courtyard.
You shall be called Peter, who denied his friend.

Words stretched out
like whipped torn taut sailcloth
across a dawning.
Chokes of sobbing you
had never known you had
and wanting him dead
rather than in their power;

if only you could kiss the dead face
tell him your shame.

A couple of hours later
eating nuts soaked in honey
needing the sweetness, gagging on it,
wanting him dead already
broken.

Words out of the future --
Their speaker, half-recognised,
standing by coals on the lakeshore,
arms wide, including.

The invitation glimpse of heaven-time:
'come and have breakfast'.

And after many thousand years
the guests were all together
on one planet – call it Uz,
call it Ariel's isle,
holding all things in common.

OTHER BOOKS FROM SHOESTRING PRESS

MORRIS PAPERS: Poems Arnold Rattenbury. Includes 5 colour illustrations of Morris's wallpaper designs. "The intellectual quality is apparent in his quirky wit and the skilful craftsmanship with which, for example, he uses rhyme, always its master, never its servant." *Poetry Nation Review.*

ISBN 1 899549 03 X £4.95

INSIDE OUTSIDE: NEW AND SELECTED POEMS Barry Cole. "A fine poet ... the real thing." *Stand.*

ISBN 1 899549 11 0 £6.95

COLLECTED POEMS Ian Fletcher. With Introduction by Peter Porter. Fletcher's work is that of "a virtuoso", as Porter remarks, a poet in love with "the voluptuousness of language" who is also a master technician.

ISBN 1 899549 22 6 £8.95

A COLD SPELL: Angela Leighton. The first full collection by a much admired poet.

ISBN: 1 899549 40 4 £6.95

TESTIMONIES: NEW AND SELECTED POEMS Philip Callow. With Introduction by Stanley Middleton. A generous selection whch brings together work from all periods of the career of this acclaimed novelist, poet and biographer.

ISBN: 1 899549 44 7 £8.95

STONELAND HARVEST: NEW AND SELECTED POEMS Dimitris Tsaloumas. This generous selection brings together poems from all periods of Tsaloumas's life and makes available for the first time to a UK readership the work of this major Greek-Australian poet.

ISBN 1 8995549 35 8 £8.00

ODES Andreas Kalvos. Translated into English by George Dandoulakis. The first English version of the work of a poet who is in some respects the equal of his contemporary, Greece's national poet, Solomos.

ISBN 1 899549 21 8 £9.95

LANDSCAPES FROM THE ORIGIN AND THE WANDERING OF YK Lydia Stephanou. Translated into English by Philip Ramp. This famous book-length poem by one of Greece's leading poets was first published in Greece in 1965. A second edition appeared in 1990.

ISBN 1 899549 20 X £8.95

POEMS Manolis Anagnostakis. Translated into English by Philip Ramp. A wide-ranging selection from a poet who is generally regarded as one of Greece's most important living poets and who in 1985 won the Greek State Prize for Poetry.

ISBN 1 899549 19 6

THE FREE BESIEGED AND OTHER POEMS Dionysios Solomos
In English versions. Edited by Peter Mackridge.

ISBN 1 899549 41 2 £8.00

SELECTED POEMS Tassos Denegris. Translated into English by Philip Ramp. A generous selection of the work of a Greek poet with an international reputation. Denegris's poetry has been translated into most major European languages and he has read across the world.

ISBN 1 899549 45 9 £6.95

THE FIRST DEATH Dimitris Lyacos. Translated into English by Shorsha Sullivan. With six masks by Friedrich Unegg. Praised by the Italian critic Bruno Rosada for "the casting of emotion into an analytical structure and its distillation into a means of communication", Lyacos's work has already made a significant impact across Europe, where it has been performed in a number of major cities.

ISBN 1 899549 42 0 £6.95

Books of related interest from Trent Editions

Robert Bloomfield: *The Selected Poems of Robert Bloomfield*

Edited by John Goodridge and John Lucas, Intro. by John Lucas

Robert Bloomfield (1766–1823), was the most successful of the self-taught 'peasant poets' of the Romantic period, a prolific and popular writer whose first book *The Farmer's Boy* (1800), sold an unprecedented 26,000 copies in three years, and won the praise of Wordsworth, and John Clare, who called him the 'English Theocritus'. In the 20th century Edmund Blunden, among others, was a great admirer of Bloomfield. This edition includes a selection of Bloomfield's prose prefaces, as well as explanatory notes, a chronology of Bloomfield's life and a list of further reading.

Price: £7.99 ISBN 0 905 48894 6

William Barnes: *The Poems of William Barnes*

Edited, with a critical commentary, by Val Shepherd

William Barnes (1801–1886) is justly renowned for poems which, using their own Dorset dialect, speak out for the agricultural labouring families of the nineteenth-century Blackmoor Vale. Many of these expressions of village and private life appear in this Trent Edition but, in addition, a selection of the little known poems that Barnes wrote in Standard English is also included.

Price: £7.99 ISBN 0 905 48895 4

John Clare: ***John Clare: the Living Year***

Edited, with an introduction and notes, by Tim Chilcott.

1841 was one of the most productive, varied, and imaginatively moving periods of John Clare's long poetic career. Against a background of asylum, escape home, and then forced removal to a second asylum, he wrote during this single year over 3,000 lines of original poetry and paraphrase, in addition to a substantial body of prose.

Price: £7.99 ISBN 0 905 488 55 5

from GREENWICH EXCHANGE

WILDERNESS: 36 POEMS 1972–93 Martin Seymour-Smith. Admired by other poets from Robert Graves to Ian Hamilton, Martin Seymour-Smith was a poet of unfailing craft who combined an astringent wit with a deep regard for the joys and pains of being alive.

ISBN 1 871551 08 0 £6.00

All these books may be ordered through Shoestring Press, 19 Devonshire Avenue, Beeston, Nottingham NG9 1BS. Tele/fax 0115 9251827.